YEMI ADEDEJI

MOVE

INTO

POSITION

CREATING TAILOR-MADE RELATIONSHIPS
TO CONNECT AND INFLUENCE

MOVE
INTO
POSITION

*Creating tailor-made relationships
to connect and influence*

YEMI ADEDEJI

Copyright ISBN: 1907095128
ISBN-13: 978-1907095122

Published by:
WINNING FAITH Outreach Ministries

London . New York . Lagos

COMMENDATIONS

Yemi has written from first-hand experience of working with people of different cultures and nations in the grace of God and maximising his opportunities. What he has learnt from first-hand experience of working directly with people in the field makes the whole book very rich with authority beyond theory.

He has not found and used an opportunity for his personal gain but a means of helping and blessing others. These experiences have been put together in a collection of steps to follow in placing persons who wish to serve in making effort to identifying strategic positions and using them to achieve maximum results.

I am impressed with Yemi's approach in encouraging those who follow in these steps to defeat timidity while remaining humble, seeking partnership with sincerity of purpose and intentionally reaching out to other organisations to achieve maximum effect. He emphasises strategy in all approach not neglecting a living relationship with God who cares even more for those we are called to serve and care for.

I commend this book first to younger persons with a serious desire to help and serve communities in need, they will grow and make the best use of this book.

I commend it to those older already in service but struggling with their work. This book is just in time and on point to get such persons out of routine to an exciting journey. I further commend it to schools of higher learning to train people on the job and new comers on the subject matter.

His Grace The Most Reverend Dr. Ben Kwashi Bishop of the Anglican Diocese of Jos and Archbishop of the Ecclesiastical Province of Jos in the Church of Nigeria.

'Yemi Adedeji's book Move into Position brilliantly illustrates how local churches can help those people most in need in the community by building strategic relationships. I recommend you buy it, read it and pass it on!'

Matt Bird, Founder of Cinnamon Network UK.

"Move into position" is a treasure of Godly wisdom born out of practical experience and inspired by a desire to motivate ones generation to attain their potential. Developing relationships and connecting with the right bodies is a Herculean task for many.

However Yemi whom I call "Mr. Relationship" has meticulously laid down practical tested principles that will make it easy for anyone who desires to move into the right position of greatness. A must read for all who aspire for greatness.

Kingsley Appiagyei
Senior Pastor Trinity Baptist Church London
and Accra and former President, Baptist Union
of Great Britain.

I can't think of anyone better qualified to write a book on this subject! Yemi is a consummate networker, so for anyone with an interest in learning about developing networks and effectiveness, this will be a must have-read. Yemi will guide you through what it takes to understand the skills and challenges from his own journey. A journey that has resulted in him becoming such an efficient and effective practician for the causes he's chosen to align with. He does it with integrity, professionalism and a good measure of fun, an altogether very important component. The fact that he's the snappiest dresser I know helps too! Read it, enjoy it and learn much.

Ian Hamilton, CEO Compassion UK

Most of us aspire to be people of influence in the context into which God has placed us. "Move into Position" by my dear friend and colleague Yemi Adedeji provides us with practical wisdom and inspiring examples of how to turn those aspirations into lives and organisations which are more likely to fulfil their God given calling. With loads of respect and appreciation.

Steve Clifford
General Director, Evangelical Alliance UK.

A diverse book that combines personal experiences with faith and life. Yemi has really brought home the good old aphorism that "If we truly endeavour to cultivate a habit of creativity in small things, creativity on a large scale will follow and definitely enhance our raison d'être."

Richie Dayo Johnson, Speaker and Experiential Coach

There are some people you meet that are larger than life and passionate about what they do. Yemi is one such individual. I've had the privilege of working alongside Yemi over the last 4 years; his endless enthusiasm and engagement in bringing about change for the sake of the Gospel is found within this book. Yemi's practical insights on managing relationships and causing them to flourish is an exciting and challenging ministry. Yemi embraces diversity and cultural context, but with a clear focus. The shared wisdom in this book, written in an engaging style should enhance every leader's ministry and effectively translate in more flourishing for the

Kingdom of God. It is both personal, practical and helpful.

Roy Crowne, Executive Director, HOPE

Having observed Yemi Adedeji at work over many years, developing strategic relationships and sustainable partnerships across cultural, ethnic, political and religious divides, I am happy to recommend this work as an authentic expression of a philosophy that works for organisations and individuals who are yet to realise their full potential.

Bishop Dr Wayne Malcolm

Move Into Position

DEDICATION

This book is dedicated to the women in my life: my dearest mother, Omoba Elizabeth Mosunmola Adedeji (nee Gbadebo) of Abeokuta, Nigeria, my dearest wife Sindeleoluwa, and my lovely daughters, Ebunoluwa, Mayowa, Oluwaseun and Elizabeth.

It is also dedicated to my only brother and buddy, Prince Adebayo Ade Adedeji.

ACKNOWLEDGMENTS

It was a sunny afternoon at the Movenpick Hotel in Accra Ghana when I sat face to face with him. I asked him to review my current situation in life and give me an honest opinion.

He looked me straight in the eye. "Yemi," he said, "you're doing a lot of things across different spheres, but I see no evidence of replication or lasting fruitfulness. What would happen to all the secrets of your good work if you were to die today?"

He paused and looked at me. "Get them down in a book," he said. "Your books will go places where you may never travel." He stood up and left.

For the next thirty minutes I sat bewildered. I felt deflated by his words, but also challenged by them. They made me determined to make a difference.

I salute you, Agu Irukwu, for helping the dream of this book to become a reality. And I'm grateful to the many people who have travelled with me on the journey. I'm grateful to Sade Kaffo, my first editor, for committing many days to travelling and sitting with me and pushing me to the finish line.

My assistants and destiny helpers are too numerous to mention. I'm grateful to them and to all my contributors whose stories and testimonies have brought this book to life. Many thanks to my children — my first critics and biggest encouragers — and to my dear wife for allowing me to flourish and do what God has called me to do.

Above all I give thanks to Almighty God for giving the grace, the gift and the life to be fruitful.

FOREWORD

Sometimes you are asked to write a foreword for a book and you can do just that, concentrating on the book. In this case I feel I would be doing a great disservice to the reader and the book if I didn't write a few sentences about the author Yemi Adedeji.

Yemi is a very colourful , engaging, passionate, bold and intelligent person. He is one of those people who is very comfortable "in his own skin". The many and varied jobs he has undertaken and roles he has served in has created a reservoir of knowledge of many topics especially as it relates to the Church and para church organisations that is enviable. From early days as a model, to working with one of the oldest missions agencies the Church Mission Society and eventually serving on its board of trustees; being ordained an Anglican clergy ; serving in the leadership of Victory Christian Centre which was one of the most vibrant churches in the city of London ;

as a pastor at Jesus House The Redeemed Christian Church of God; as a director of the One people commission of the evangelical alliance; on the boards of several para church ministries including Compassion UK and HOPE, Yemi has garnered so much information on his topic and that is what makes this book compelling .

Now to the book, from the first page the purpose is clear and I would have been surprised if it was any other way, knowing the author. In a very simple, easy to follow and practical style the book encourages persons and organisations, especially local churches to be more effective in engaging with the communities in which they are. Yemi's passion for the local church to be "salt and light" to its world is very clear as you read the book. Whilst his target audience is not limited, it is obvious that he has a burden for the ethnic minority churches that seek to engage across cultural barriers that can sometimes seem insurmountable. Getting those who have implemented some of these strategies successfully to tell their own stories in the book allows us to hear other voices buttressing the points he makes.

I am privileged to know all those stories and was

immensely encouraged to read about them. One of the highlights of the book is that it is really a manual, a "how to" book. Having been opportuned to be a part of Yemi' s life for quite a while, I am so glad that he has put pen to paper to do what he is so passionate about, encourage individuals and organisations to have a greater impact and influence for the kingdom of God in their worlds. I would recommend this book for anyone who wants to do that. I would especially recommend it to the many pastors of largely migrant or ethnic minority churches who desire to be more relevant in their communities.

Agu Irukwu
Senior Pastor, Jesus House
Head, Redeemed Christian Church of God UK

CONTENTS

Move Into Position

INTRODUCTION

Most people want to do something worthwhile that will influence their community and advance their work. However, because they've not been able to develop strategic relationships with external bodies, organisations and government agencies, their fruitfulness has been limited. In fact, they may have ended up as little more than bench warmers.

This has led to frustration, prejudice and a siege mentality for many people and their leaders, especially those who are minorities or migrants or who are starting a new initiative within a relatively new territory.

This book will highlight simple ways and ideas that have been tried, tested and developed through experience. It will show how individuals, church leaders, external bodies, organisations and government agencies, big and small, can become voices in their community and major players of influence.

People will discover how to develop strategic relationships with bodies and organisations. They will also identify their areas of competency and learn how to become leaders who will influence their community and city.

Yemi Adedeji

Move Into Position

ONE

80/20 dynamics asserts that 80% of results will come from 20% of effort.

WHY WORK WITH OTHERS?

A few years ago I launched out as an entrepreneur, providing a service I am passionate about. My first mistake was to think I could do this on my own, without support or assistance. But as I explored ways to make the business work, I realised it couldn't succeed unless I formed intentional and strategic relationships.

So I explored my areas of strength and competency but also looked at the gaps that needed to be filled by other skill sets. I didn't want to struggle on in areas where I had no capability. Instead I sought to work with others who had the talents I lacked.

Partnerships like these enable individuals, organisations and institutions to make continuous improvements and keep on growing. A partnership succeeds when two or more people share resources and competencies for a common good, for a cause that can benefit all parties.

The 80/20 Dynamic

The 80/20 Dynamic asserts that 80 percent of results come from 20 percent of effort. In order to achicvc more with less, you must be selective without being exhaustive.

In every sphere of work you need to work out where 20 percent of effort can lead to 80 percent of return, while you strive for excellence in a few key areas.

It's better to excel in these few areas than to settle for "good" in many areas of your performance. Being in partnership allows you to focus your resources on what *you* do best. Meanwhile, you can tap into the resources of others who can do some other things better. In this way you will all create a sustainable competitive advantage.

In one of my engagements with a particular organisation whose aim was to raise sponsors to help children out of poverty, I applied the 80/20 rule. Over a period of 24 months we were able to get sponsors for more than 2000 poor children around the world. Knowing how complex the whole process was, I simply focused on my own area of competency.

I used my 20 percent effort to find and build relationships with potential sponsors, while colleagues whose gifts were in facilitation, administration and marketing contributed their 80 percent across other functions, roles and responsibilities.

When deciding why, when, how and who to partner with for complementary support or aid, you need to evaluate the time you invest in less important tasks against an investment of time that will have long-term results.

Working with others is about finding a common ground to agree on a Yes, and working through differences when there is a No. In simple terms, partnership must be seen as a collaborative agreement between two or more parties with the aim of:

- Working together to achieve a common purpose,
- Undertaking a specific task,
- Sharing risks, responsibilities, resources, competencies and benefits.

Unless these three things happen, you are unlikely to move beyond a "partnership dream" to create meaningful change. The language of partnership implies that each stakeholder, group or individual has something to contribute and some way to benefit by being involved.

Partnership means different things to different people

The reality is that each stakeholder will have a different perception of their personal benefits.

Churches are an important area for partnerships. They enable unity to be promoted across a movement, and they can result in greater co-operation and improved understanding. If ecumenical partnerships are to be genuinely transformative and meaningful they must consciously address the aspects of "working across differences" and "finding common ground."

Without both processes, it is unlikely that they can create meaningful change. "Working across differences" is a process of naming, mapping, and working with our differences, whether they relate to experience, ability, race, class, or gender.

Working with others is about finding a common ground to agree on a Yes, and working through differences when there is a No.

Getting to "yes" is about finding strength in our differences, not by simply assuming common needs and experience. The latter can have a numbing effect on the group process. So finding common ground and engaging in ecumenism is "filtered through" our differences and strengths.

God: An example of partnership in creation

God the Father created and continues to relate to his creation in partnership and in relationship with his Son Jesus Christ and with the Holy Spirit. The term

Trinity defines God as three constitutional persons, expressed as the Father, the Son and the Holy Spirit. They are distinct but of "one substance, essence and nature."

The partners here are co-equal and co-powerful and clearly strategic when engaging with humanity. For example, God the Father picked us out for himself before the foundation of the world (Ephesians 1:4), God the Son redeemed us from our sins (Ephesians 1:7), and God the Holy Spirit sealed the promise of God the Father and the redemption of God the Son. (Ephesians 1:13)

God could have created the world and redeemed humanity by himself, but he showed the power of partnership and relationship in a strategic way. The persons of the Godhead, though distinct in their co-existence, are united as one for a purpose.

CASE STUDY
A church that benefited and influenced its community through partnerships with other organisations

Harvest Fellowship, Rugby, UK,
by Morola Hayden

I think the major breakthrough in the acceptance of our church by the community came when the church formed a partnership with *HOPE Together*.

This is a catalyst organisation that brings churches together to transform communities in the UK. It supports UK churches to do mission together in word and deed.

Our Story

We started a partnership with HOPE Together when it was officially launched as an organisation by the General Overseer of our denomination. This happened at the denomination's biannual gathering, an event which signifies a corporate belonging and partnership of common purpose, although each church within the denomination is different in context, background, orientation and operation. Without doubt such a partnership at the top level was strategic. It became the turning point for all the churches within our denomination in the UK.

At our church "Harvest Fellowship," we rode the wave of this corporate partnership, expressed in context within our local community. We are still riding this wave. It has developed into various relationships that are strategic on many fronts.

Since HOPE Together's head office is in Rugby, our local town made the partnership famous. It was a great opportunity that later grew into an authentic relationship and partnership across many fronts.

How we leveraged for benefits

We set out by first inviting the head of HOPE Together to visit and interact with our congregation. We requested him to speak at our services and conferences, as a first step towards developing a relationship around fellowship, food and drinks.

In our journey towards developing a strategic partnership, this achieved two things.

First, it helped our congregation, who are predominantly black and African in background, to understand and appreciate the mandate of the church. It invigorated their individual commitment to engage with a new community. And it modelled our commitment to the leaders of our denomination as they embraced and engaged in several HOPE initiatives. The corporate message for our churches was simply to embrace the initiative as part of God's agenda and his divine vehicle to integrate our ethnic churches into the fabric of the United Kingdom.

The step change

The church members now saw themselves as part of the bigger picture. They fulfilled the expectation to take their place in partnering with the various initiatives that HOPE brought within the local Christian community, and it wasn't long before our church became a voice to be heard and listened to.

This certainly encouraged the congregation and helped many of its ethnic minority members to connect in various ways to foster partnership and develop relationships.

The second benefit was the *value* derived from the relationship. Soon people began to take notice of us as a church. The community could affirm the work we were doing among various people groups. As a result people saw the ongoing relevance of our work and in Rugby we solidified our position as one of the town's many thriving churches.

Positive outcome

Our church is now community-focused, with projects aimed at serving our neighbours. We set up a junior school, we embraced the CAP (Christian Against Poverty) initiative, and ran a job club which has been very successful. (Five of our members found jobs through it).

TWO

Similar to "One World" fast growing organisations must rely heavily on alliances

THE UNIQUENESS OF STRATEGIC RELATIONSHIPS

Individuals, organisations and churches will end up entering into one or another form of partnership over the course of their existence. They will do this in order to achieve growth and develop capacity in the areas in which they are less competent.

A strategic relationship, as distinct from a normal partnership, creates a formal coalition between two or more parties wherein each party possesses one or more advantages that will help the other. It is a relationship in which one of the parties either lacks the capacity to deliver in a certain area or chooses not to develop this capacity internally, since it can readily benefit from the competency of the other party. Usually it takes more than one person or organisation to effect influence.

Narrative of three churches working in strategic relationship
Over a period of three years, three key churches in the UK formed a strategic relationship in order to achieve a cohesive front that would cut across the city of London. Their goal was to deliver an event of major influence ("The Pentecost Celebration") that would have been impossible to achieve if each had tried to do it separately.

Organising the event involved a strategic partnership that could plan, programme, draw in people, and provide for corporate and individual input and the final execution. It was an alliance that allowed each party to relinquish areas of incompetency and advance areas of particular ability. Holy Trinity Brompton, one of the largest Anglican churches, came with various competences of worship and organisation that expressed its English context.

Hillsong, which originated in Australia, belonged to the worldwide denomination of the Assemblies of God. The competencies it brought included young, vibrant Caucasian followers from different nationalities, a dynamic worship team and a high volume of members and supporters. The ability of the church to attract other Caucasians of non-English backgrounds created a unique space.

Usually it takes more than one person or organisation to effect influence.

Jesus House, London, was the third party in the strategic relationship, and its contributions to the final mix created a formidable front. Jesus House is the premier parish of the largest black/ethnic denomination in the UK. The Redeemed Christian Church of God is populated largely by Africans in diaspora, whose charismatic and Pentecostal expression is evident in their gospel choir and music.

The programme allowed leaders from each group to make a presentation in the primary area of their competence. The vicar of the Holy Trinity parish of the Anglican Church delivered an exhortation that was simple yet provocative, inspiring and thoughtful. The senior pastor of the Jesus House parish of the worldwide Redeemed Christian Church of God challenged people to worship God not only in praise but also with the resources God had blessed them with. The leading pastor of Hillsong UK, of the Assemblies of God movement, challenged people without apology to commit to following Jesus as their Lord and Saviour.

It was this cohesive front and joint collaboration that enabled such historic events to be staged across key venues in the city of London over a period of three years.

Strategic Alliances : Why and How to Build Them
A strategic relationship happens when two or more organisations or individuals join together for a set period of time. Such individuals or organisations will not usually be in direct competition, but will serve the same target audience.

In an alliance people cooperate with others to produce a better result. Because the church and the general population continue to evolve, alliances help them to make continuous advancements.

Strategic partnerships between individuals and organisations allow them to share resources, capabilities, and core competencies and ultimately to pursue mutual interests. Such partnerships or alliances can be structured in various ways, depending on their purpose.

1. Stand-alone Strategic Partnerships

These may be developed through individuals, small businesses or organisations that seek to work with others on a personal level. Churches may work in relationship with other churches for mutual benefit and advantage. An example was seen when Jesus House UK, from the RCCG Pentecostal denomination, was working with Holy Trinity Brompton, an Anglican parish. Such a partnership allowed the two organisations to share resources and skills to achieve a common purpose. This was demonstrated in many ways, a good example being when the two churches came together to offer each other specific services.

Holy Trinity Brompton, which pioneered the Alpha courses, offered to help Jesus House to expand their evangelism strategy within the English postmodern context, while Jesus House partnered with HTB to help them develop a deeper prayer life. Such a stand-alone strategic relationship allowed each organisation to benefit from the other as competencies were exchanged and benefits were derived across the board.

2. Denominational or Organisational Strategic Partnerships

Denominations may work in partnership with other denominations. For example, the Anglican denomination may work in partnership with the Methodist movement or Baptists may work in partnership with Pentecostals. In the corporate world, an example is seen when a corporation such as British Airways works in a strategic partnership with Iberia as part of the One Alliance group. From a business perspective, it is obvious that the airlines belonging to the One Alliance group do not all fly to the same destination. But the alliance allows customers to book with any of the airlines within the group and receive the benefits available to all of them. The partnership allows many destinations to be routed, thereby allowing travelers a wider choice and ultimately attracting more customers.

I remember an occasion when I was due to fly out to Malabo in Equatorial Guinea. My airline of choice did not fly to Malabo. But the benefit of an alliance paid off because the airline I eventually flew with, Iberia, permitted me to purchase my ticket from

British Airways and gave me all the benefits of BA's flying club membership.

3. Joint Venture Strategic Alliances

An alliance made with another body or union for a common purpose allows the organisations to have a strong, united agenda. This helps especially when the organisations wish to put pressure on a government body or advocate for new initiatives.

Because the church and the general population continue to evolve, alliances help them to make continuous advancements.

Examples are seen in alliances between charitable organisations such as the Evangelical Alliance, Hope Together UK, Christian Aid, and Compassion UK. Such alliances allow member organisations to enjoy corporate benefits and support, especially when looking for acknowledgment and certification.

There are also corporate organisations in which individuals and organisations strategically belong to a group, a body or a union for competitive advantage and advocacy.

Why is strategic partnership important?

In the postmodern world, strategic alliances enable individuals and organisations to benefit from access to the partners' resources, including their networks, technologies, funding, and people. Teaming up with others adds complementary resources and capabilities, enabling individuals, churches and organisations to grow and expand rapidly and efficiently.

Fast-growing organisations rely heavily on alliances to improve their operational outcomes. Individual organisations don't need to reinvent things, or develop processes from scratch, so they can be free to focus on innovation and their signature giftings.

Many fast-growing churches and businesses need strategic alliances so they can benefit from established channels and networks of credible and well-known players. Migrant churches are growing, as are networks in diaspora, and this will no doubt increase both their competition and their prominence.

So mid-size churches, businesses and networks operating in diaspora must be creative in their linkages, choosing how and with whom they will align themselves for growth and development.

CASE STUDY
Hillingdon Foodbank, London UK,
by Tunde Balogun

The Hillingdon Foodbank provides short-term, nutritionally-balanced food to families in the borough who are going through crises. The Hillingdon Foodbank is built on compassion, integrity and a commitment to restore dignity and give hope. It works in partnership with voluntary and statutory agencies which come into contact with people in emergency situations. When it was launched in March 2009, Hillingdon was the first foodbank in London.

Food is donated by individuals, schools, churches and organizations. Volunteers collect food from supermarkets, individuals, churches, schools and other organizations. This is then sorted, banked, and prepared for distribution to those in need.

Our church's role in advancing Foodbank
Whenever I hear about Foodbank it reminds me of the sheer determination and commitment of our

local congregation, Kingsborough Family Church, to use what we had as an outreach tool for our community to extend God's Kingdom. I am always humbled and filled with gratitude.

What I saw

One fateful evening as we were getting ready to head back to London after visiting friends in Suffolk, I was standing at the front door for another last minute chat. Suddenly I looked up and noticed a little girl, about ten years old, running across the road opposite me. She was wearing a white tee-shirt with FOODBANK emblazoned across the front. As I continued talking to my host I couldn't stop thinking about that little girl. After about twenty minutes I asked my host, "What is Foodbank?" Sam, my host, gave me a quick rundown on the activity of the Haverhill Foodbank. It was part of a network of projects seeded from the Trussel Trust in Salisbury, UK.

God spoke

There and then, I heard God speak to my heart. I needed to take the Foodbank project to Uxbridge which was within my local borough of Hillingdon in London. In short, I felt that Foodbank would be one of the next vehicles, God would use to glorify himself across the United Kingdom.

We got home late that night, but by morning I had researched the Internet to find out all I needed to know about Foodbank. I was ready to contact the Trussel Trust, who had birthed Foodbank, to ask them how I might follow up what I felt I'd heard from God.

Fast-growing organisations rely heavily on alliances to improve their operational outcomes.

The next morning I called the head office of the Trussel Trust in Salisbury, and spoke to the person who was the national director of the Foodbank project at the time. *How could we start this project in Uxbridge?* I wanted to know. His polite response had a cynical undertone. In our long chat that morning, he patiently explained to me in more detail the mission of Foodbank. He mentioned how many other people had called from London in the past, just as I was doing, adding that, sadly, nothing had ever come from these enquiries.

There were two reasons for this. First, most people who called to enquire had decided Foodbank was not needed in London; its residents were not seen as deprived enough to need such a service. In other words, there were "no hungry people in London."

Secondly, the amount of work involved in getting such a project up and running seemed so overwhelming that most callers gave up without even trying. In response, I told the then CEO of Foodbank that my enquiry was born out of a passion, conviction and directive from God. I reiterated that if God had indeed put this into my heart as a vehicle of revival in London, he would surely make it work.

Beginning a Strategic Partnership
After much deliberation, we initiated a plan to get the churches in Uxbridge together to launch the project. In March 2009 we set up an evening meeting where seventeen churches came together to hear my story. I told them how I'd been inspired in Suffolk by a little girl who was wearing a tee-shirt inscribed with the name *Foodbank*. The then CEO also shared his vision with the group, describing what would be involved in setting up the first Foodbank in London.

Unfortunately, only a few of the church leaders present shared my enthusiasm for this new project, since Uxbridge was generally seen as an affluent, middle class community. But I was convinced I had heard from God, and proceeded to forge an agreement with the Trussel Trust. I decided that if no other church was willing to get behind the project, our "Kingsborough Family Church" would take it on. (At that time Kingsborough, in the London borough of Hillingdon, was the first and only parish of my denomination, "the Redeemed Christian Church of God.")

To that end we set aside Saturday, 14 March, 2009, as the first day of our Hillingdon Foodbank food collection, at the Tesco supermarket on Uxbridge's main street. This event attracted important dignitaries including the local councillors, civic leaders and even the mayor of Hillingdon. In my experience, the birth of the Hillingdon Foodbank stood out as an exceptional way to engage the local community, and we launched it as we would launch any other community project.

Regardless of the demography of a given community or the diversity of its projects, the principles remain the same. And they will work every time, if we follow the proven pattern of engagement and delivery. Contrary to people's doubts about the challenges we might face, the Hillingdon Foodbank was warmly welcomed by the community. It was seen as a safety net to help people who were caught in the crisis enveloping the nation as a result of the credit crunch.

No sooner had the Hillingdon Foodbank opened, than the soaring number of clients came to the attention of the civic authorities. By May 2010, the Hillingdon Foodbank had been given the status of Mayoral Charity of the Year by his worship, the mayor of Hillingdon.

We continued to provide services that benefited the general community, regardless of faith, culture, race, age or sex. Seventy percent of the clients were also issued vouchers directly from the borough council, or designated departments of the council. Churches, local businesses, schools, GP surgeries and other community groups became the arms of the Hillingdon Foodbank to reach out and provide services to those who needed the service daily.

In order to maintain the unprecedented success that Foodbank was achieving as a Christian charity in our London borough, it became apparent that the church needed to put in place effective channels and mechanisms to gather future strategic partners for engagement.

It is important to note that strategic partners sometimes change, depending on the desires and interests of the partners at different points in time. From our experience, the focus of churches and organizations does not always allow them to continue engaging as they had done at first. Expectations have to be managed well, so that even when some partners draw back as a result of needing to give priority to more pressing in-house issues, they may well be able to resume their support later. So when a partnership involves a financial contribution, it is important to remember that the interest, focus, goals and mission of that group may vary, as does its capacity to provide resources.

The Foodbanks have multiplied in the London area and there are now more than a hundred projects supported by the central Trussel Trust. But certain principles are essential for the success of any individual, church or organisation wanting to engage in community ministries that provide support and comfort for vulnerable people.

In my experience, the following principles helped us to be effective:

1. We discovered our entry and connection point

There is an entry point waiting for everyone who wants to connect with their community. This is not the same for everyone. It is directly related to your unique gifts, passions, skills, interests and work.

2. We had a specific vision and purpose

Don't go into the community without understanding the who, what, when, where and how of your purpose and vision. People will remember you for your clarity of purpose and the vision and attributes you bring. You will gain influence by offering to help in areas of your gifts and skills.

3. We developed a network of relationships

There are always like minds and complementary visions among existing relationships. The key is to find these and align with them. The strength of your relationships determines the value and level of your influence.

4. We were compassionate

Compassion binds you to solutions. When you connect to your community from a solution standpoint, you will complain less, you will be less judgmental, and you will pray more.

5. We tried to be true ambassadors of the kingdom

We tried to exemplify good values (excellence, time keeping, integrity, transparency) among ourselves and in our work. Once we started working with the community we noticed we were no longer hidden. We became visible across the town.

6. We did a survey of our community

It is important to gather knowledge about your community and its needs. It is only when you find out more about the past, the prevailing situation and the future plans of your community that you gain insights into it. Nothing is revealed on the surface. A deep and conscious look into what seems ordinary may reveal a new way to facilitate engagement and support that will help move the community forward.

Move Into Position

THREE

Never engage in partnership empty-handed but from a position or place of specific competency or service of what you have that will give you what you want.

CHAPTER 3

THE RULES OF ENGAGEMENT

I was once invited to a meeting of top leaders to discuss a new initiative, and the key issues as they affected people, communities and businesses. The contributions offered by the participants were on a high level, well above the constituency I was representing. Noting the way the meeting was going, I realized I needed to be clear about the uniqueness of my offer and what would eventually make a positive difference to the constituency I was representing.

First, I suggested to the meeting two areas of competitive advantage that might apply to my constituency. I offered to launch the proposed initiative at one of our gatherings, which was a major

59

assembly of tens of thousands of people. It wasn't long before all the plans were being shaped around my offer and I ended up becoming the key player, although I was only offering a venue for the launch.

Secondly, I proposed an activity that would involve a large number of participants during the launch. By not engaging empty-handed, and by bringing to the table my area of competency, I could swing the nucleus of the initiative in the direction I had in mind. I did not need to draw attention to what I was less skilled at or what my constituency could not offer.

Simply the rules are:

1. Do not engage in strategic partnerships empty-handed.

2. Always position yourself or your organisation from the place of your specific competency or service.

Many individuals, organisations and churches enter into a partnership without a clear understanding of their competency or what they already possess for competitive negotiation. The rule of the game is never to engage empty-handed, or as a beggar, but to be aware of the value that already exists within.

A small church engaging with a bigger church or large organisation might want to consider its inherent gift areas. What skills does it have that the partner lacks? Examples could range from generic to specific, such as the church's prayer team. An individual or organisation might also be able to offer space as a value or area of competency.

Successful people invest their time, energy and resources into their core strengths because that is where they get the highest return.

Before entering into a strategic alliance, you need to think carefully about the structure of the proposed relationship and how it will be managed.

In your planning process:
- Define the expected outcomes of the relationship for all the parties in the strategic alliance
- Define and document the elements provided by each party, and the benefits a successful alliance brings to each

- Identify the results that will cause the alliance to be most beneficial for your organisation and define the structure and operating issues that need to be addressed to achieve these results
- Protect your organisation's intellectual property rights through legal agreements and restrictions when transferring information.
- Define the basis of how you will operate
- Be certain that cultures are compatible or complimentary, and that the parties can operate with an acceptable level of trust

When advising individuals and groups in Corinth, the apostle Paul spoke about the different gifts that were given to believers. Through collaboration and individual input, a powerful outcome could be achieved.

"There are diversities of gifts..." 1 Corinthians 12:4 NKJV

Successful people invest their time, energy and resources into their core strengths because that is where they get the highest return. But some people ignore that wisdom, as Colin Salmon did when he took time out from his successful acting career to participate in the BBC's *Strictly Come Dancing*. Colin, a statuesque, confident actor proved to be less competent in the dancing arena, leaving the show after just five weeks and never receiving higher than 27 points from the panel of judges. He may have enjoyed the experience, but exiting the show so early is probably not what he'd like to be remembered for.

CASE STUDY
Revival Christian Church Enfield
by Nick Chanda

I would like to share how strategic partnerships and alliances have worked for us. As a small church and growing organisation, we understood the principle of not approaching a partnership empty handed, and we brought three key things to the table, namely prayer, a church bus and our church building.

The Revival Christian Church of Enfield is a small, growing church that began in May, 2009. Two weeks after we started as church, we were invited to a meeting of church leaders to plan Hope Enfield 2009, a citywide outreach, and during the meeting all the churches highlighted what skills and resources they could contribute. Our contribution was morning prayer from 6am to 7am for five days at the venue of the outreach, plus a free mini-bus for transportation. Hope Enfield 2009 was a success as we saw the youth being transported to various corners of the borough to conduct effective outreach. Hope Enfield 2009 introduced us to various strategic partners such as New River church, Chace Family Church, Nflame, Edmonton Baptist church, etc.

We now have a strategic alliance with the Nflame Youth group. Nflame conducts leadership and evangelism training (LET) every year. In 2006 I was invited to lead some training at their annual conference and have done so every year since. In 2011 Nflame conducted LET training in our church building. As part of the partnership arrangement we offered prayer and a free minibus to Nflame and they offered in return LET training and Gap year student training. We have been able to draw strength from each other along the way.

Through opening our church building for ministers' breakfasts, we are now positioned as one of the representatives of Enfield at the London Network of Networks which comprises 32 boroughs of London. We recently did a joint advert at the train station with another church, New River. We have also developed a strategic relationship with the Enfield Faith Forum where we managed to find new community partners such as the Enfield Credit Union whom we hosted for their Annual General Meeting. We also hosted their finance training for the community and some of our members received training as well.

In 2009 Noah's Ark, a children's hospice, had a meeting with their fundraising managers in our building. We deepened our strategic relationship by offering our bus to them whenever they needed to transport the hospice children and their families. This resulted in a strategic community partnership. Each time transport was needed for the families of terminally ill children, we provided free transport and a driver.

We were awarded a certificate as key supporters of their organisation, and this helped us to obtain planning permission from the council for our church building. We found we were able to engage people whom we would have had no chance to meet on the street. Since then the bus has been offered, as a strategic competence advantage, to various other organisations and groups.

Our gift of prayer has opened doors to us in the Houses of Parliament. Over the years we have attended various prayer initiatives in Parliament and were recently invited as a church by our MP, David

Burrowes, to tour the Houses of Parliament and offer prayers for the lawmakers. Our experience of strategic partnership so far has taught us that sharing resources reduces costs, strengthens networks, and continually opens doors to work with new partners.

FOUR

Always aim to progress from being a participant to becoming a worthwhile contributor and ultimately a key player leading in a management position

THE DYNAMICS OF STRATEGIC ENGAGEMENT

When engaging in strategic relationships your goal must be to become an organisation or individual of influence, positioned as a strategic player in your community or sphere of operation.

You must aim to progress from being just a participant to being a worthwhile contributor and key player, and ultimately a player in management. Engaging in various forms of relationships is great but the ultimate aim for an individual or an organisation is to influence their sphere, community or city. You go from participant to key player to team manager. How well you succeed in this will be evident in the number of people from your organisation who are representatives and players across all decision-making bodies. The intentional positioning of volunteers, players and influencers on major boards and leading groups is what steers key initiatives within the local setting.

Your aim is not just to be elected to sit on planning or management boards across the community. While being appointed to a board is a laudable first step towards becoming a contributor and player among the decision-makers, nothing compares to becoming a leader of the group. This is influence at its best! Many churches have mastered this dynamic of relational engagement, and have registered their presence strongly within specified areas.

Things to consider when aiming to become a player in a management position
1. Organic growth alone will not make your organisation or church relevant to the community if you do not have an influential voice. For the growth of lasting influence, your presence must lead to your having a voice that will advance your organisation's impact on the community.

2. Multiplying the spread of your organisation or church by replicating its initiatives is essential and greatly improves your partnership leverage, but your aim must be to influence the spiritual and social direction of the community through local participation.

3. Complexity is increasing, and no single church or organisation has all the expertise needed to best serve the public. So you need to understand your areas of gifting and the specific competencies that will enable your organisation to become a player with a management role.

4. When you venture into new initiatives, partnership with others gives you access into research already done, thus reducing your development costs. Some information is specific to particular audiences and is restricted. Such privileged information in a strategic relationship can be an advantage that opens the door to your being invited to become a player and contributor.

5. Alliances facilitate access to generic and specific funding for various projects. So cultivating strategic alliances and partnerships should become a goal of your church or organisation, in view of local, national

and global competition for funding. Specific needs that are peculiar to organisations can be pioneered in partnership to obtain grants or funding. This will ultimately create space for capacity building and for directions that will be mutually beneficial.

In summary...

In a strategic alliance, participants willingly modify their basic church and organisational practices for the purpose of reducing duplication and waste while facilitating improved performance and gaining an influential leadership role in the community. A partnership may be seen as a relationship between organisations for the purposes of implementing a strategic plan and becoming a church or an organisation of influence.

You must aim to progress from being just a participant to being a worthwhile contributor and key player, and ultimately a player in management.

If a partnership is to contribute to the successful functioning of a church or organization, it must be *strategic*. The relationship must be supported by leadership and set up by lower management at the macro level. Leadership must identify specialists who can competently represent the organisation.

Strategic alliances are not a remedy for every church and organisation in every situation. But through them churches and organisations can improve their competitive positioning, gain entry to new audiences, supplement critical skills, and share the risk and cost of major development projects.

CASE STUDY
The Anchor for All Souls and Greenwich Borough, London.
by Segun Adenuga

This is the story of how our church went beyond the four walls of its building and actively engaged the community as light bearers.

My journey into community engagement started in 2002 when my son was starting school in a predominantly Caucasian community. He, along with other non-Caucasian students, represented the minority ethnic groups in the school. Looking at the social demographics of the school, my parental instinct spurred me to participate in its decision-making body, knowing well that an opportunity to have a say on the school board would enable me to bring to the table the concerns and interests of students in minority groups.

So I decided to run for one of the positions of parent governor. I would later find out that I was the first and only black ethnic minority parent governor the school had ever had. Little did I know that I was on a journey that would take me deeper into the social composition and life of my community.

As the leader and pastor of a local church, I have always envisaged the church as being a strong voice in society. I saw the local church as a positive influence, leaving its mark on the immediate community. To this end I encouraged as many of our members as possible to find relevant roles within the community. This included being parent governors in schools, taking part in the Neighbourhood Watch, registering with a political party, getting involved in politics where possible, starting local businesses and identifying the strategic needs of the society.

For us as a church located in the Thamesmead-Bexley borough of south east London, we found that the key need of our community was a strong family structure and vibrant family life. This need was evident from the number of parents who were going to jail, not for crimes relating to theft or fraud but because of a cultural anomie in child rearing. The cultural understanding and positions of the immigrant community in the UK regarding child discipline were at variance with the laws of the land.

While parents believed they were meting out appropriate punishments to discourage bad behavior in their children, the laws of the land adjudged such punitive measures to be child abuse. So the parents were being booked, and soon many of the children were living in foster homes while concerned parents were either in jail or had been strongly warned by the authorities.

In response to this problem our church decided to put together a Safeguarding conference where parents were taught how to handle their children in ways that produced appropriate behaviour without contravening the laws of the United Kingdom. This programme was a huge success, going by the number of attendees and the results it produced in the life of the community.

Let me mention here that one of the factors contributing to the success of the programme was its presentation in conjunction with the LSBC. The conference has since become an annual event for the Bexley borough and has given the church a presence and visibility in the social life of the community.

The next stage of our community engagement targeted young persons. Because of the prevalent antisocial behaviour of teenagers in the community, we started the Anchor Summer Teenage and Kids Club. The idea was to equip kids of all ages and races with needed social skills, ethics and manners. We wanted to help them become socially fit, culturally adjusted, manually dexterous, spiritually aware and morally sound individuals who could participate effectively in a merit-oriented and egalitarian society.

What we do in the Summer Kids Club is bring potential mentors and life tutors who can challenge and inspire young kids to aspire to a great future. We design age-based pedagogical and social activities that enable them to bond and interact together. We've been amazed and blessed by the testimonies of parents who tell us over and over how their kids have been transformed into youth with a mission after experiencing our summer events.

Some of the kids who have passed through our summer programmes have gone on to attend some of the best universities in the country and in other parts of the world. God be praised for making us a lighthouse in our community.

Initially our church was the sole sponsor of the Safeguarding conference, which meant a lot of financial involvement and sacrifice on our part. But as time went on and the impact of the conference grew, corporate bodies, public institutions and other local agencies who were impressed with what we were doing decided to fund it.

This is testimony to the fact that when we make a positive difference in our community, we will not lack support or provision. Jesus ministered to ten lepers and one came back to say "thank you." If we keep on ministering to the community, we can be sure that at least a percentage will come back to thank us. But more than that, we have our reward before the Lamb of God.

High crime was a major social malady in the borough where our first church was located, and most of the people involved were youth and young adults. This became another focus of our community engagement. My leaders and I met at different times to pray and strategise on how to minister effectively to our community in this respect. Although we had achieved a measure of success in reaching parents, teenagers and children, we figured a new strategy would be needed to meet the challenge of crime in the community. I remember asking God for wisdom to deal with the problem. As we began to research the community, God gave us a vital connection. A man gave us the contact of another person who happened to be one of the locals.

That man was an embodiment of the history, culture and transformation that had happened in Greenwich (our new borough). We took advantage of his knowledge of the community and his goodwill to reach out to the Metropolitan Police. Of course the police were aware of the church, as news of our various initiatives, particularly the youth conference, had reached them. And they were looking for an opportunity to be a part of what we were doing.

Integrity was a vital factor as we strove to impact our community. It is worth noting that for some partnerships or projects, reference checks had to be done on the church and its leadership. So it was imperative that the church and its leaders should maintain a lifestyle of integrity and nobility that commanded the respect of authority structures in the community. A life that was devoid of moral excellence and virtue could close the door to the community in which we ministered. So we needed to model the lifestyle we wanted the community to practice.

OnTrack, our youth initiative, grew in relevance as we began to engage with young persons to minimize their mistakes and maximise their opportunities. What of those who had at one point or another been caught in some negative social or satanic web? We sought to restore the hope found in the gospel by showing these young ones practical love and discipline, helping them to mature into the constructive personalities they had always wanted to be.

A major testimony was that of a gang member who had served several prison terms but who now, after due rehabilitation, was an associate youth leader in our local assembly. This labour of love for young people was eventually recognized. The Metropolitan Police was so struck by the transformational impact of *OnTrack* on the social landscape and youth culture of Greenwich that they invited our church to be one of the representatives on the Serious Youth Violence Panel (SYVP).

We were delighted for Anchor for All Souls to serve in this way to ensure safety for the community at large. God is no respecter of persons. If he gave us this leadership and social impact in Greenwich, we know he can give your church visibility and grace at an even higher level.

As I had served in the capacity of parent governor and on the curriculum committee years before my call to pastoral ministry, my experience of community engagement in those areas came in handy. It helped me to steer our church into membership of the Standing Advisory Committee for Religious Education (SACRE).

Your aim is not just to be elected to sit on planning or management boards across the community.

The lesson I have learned in all this is simple: if we are ready to start out from little and unseen places in the community, God will be faithful to take us to higher places of responsibility and visibility. We must first be salt to the earth (functioning in an unseen place yet making a visible impact) before we become a light to the world that cannot be hidden.

After moving the church from Bexley to Greenwich for expansion reasons, we continued to impact our local and immediate community through family-oriented programmes such as a nursery school on the church premises. We served our community by helping to take care of the infants so the adult members could go about their daily business without having to worry about the well-being of the young ones. To help raise the quality of family life in the community, we also offered post marriage counselling sessions tagged *You & I*. We opened our church property to the community for conferences, community engagements and recreation, wanting everybody in the neighbourhood to know that ours was not just a church — it was *their* church.

Having said all this, I need to mention that community engagement is not without its costs and challenges. Every church leader who wants to maximise this style of evangelisation must be ready to pay the price. Counselling, training and mentoring are all time-demanding adventures. We must be ready to have our schedule disrupted by emergencies. We must be ready to sacrifice financially. Community outreaches consume money —money that may not be obvious in the state of our church building or in the sophistication of our public address system. Sometimes we may be misunderstood by the community and/or by the brethren. That's why it's important for the pastor to clarify his or her goals for community engagement, and to communicate that vision effectively until all the members have grasped the church's purpose.

Community engagement is costly and demanding, yet it is a cardinal purpose of the church. It is like sowing in the land. What I have come to know, however, is that as we sow in the land, God will enable us to reap in due season. We shall reap the harvest of reaching out, both in time and in eternity.

The church is designed to minister to the Godhead (worship), to minister to one another (fellowship) and to minister to the world (evangelism and mission). Today, we seem to have given the right amount of attention to the first two responsibilities of the church — worship and fellowship — but have too often neglected our third responsibility — evangelism and mission.

I challenge you, my reader, to take the ministry of your church to the next level by actively engaging your community with all the resources God has committed to you. Take your church into the community!

Move Into Position

FIVE

*Never allow the pressure of instant gratification make you offer
your live chicken in exchange for an egg.*

Move Into Position

THE WISDOM OF STRATEGIC PARTNERSHIP

We must avoid the "Esau to Jacob exchange" as an engagement strategy (Genesis 25:19 - 34). I have often called this the "egg and chicken" syndrome. It's like the man who had a chicken but little or no understanding of its value and what it could produce. He despised the current state of the chicken while looking hungrily at someone else's bowl of eggs. In fact his desire for instant gratification caused him to offer his live chicken in exchange for the eggs.

He hadn't a clue that a careful nurturing of the chicken could have yielded tons of eggs to his delight and benefit. Jacob was boiling pottage (lentil stew)

87

one day, when Esau came in from the field, feeling faint with hunger. Esau said to Jacob, "I beg you, let me have some of that red lentil stew to eat, for I am famished!" That is why he was called Edom [red].

Jacob answered, "Then sell me today your birthright (the rights of a firstborn)." Esau said, "Look, I'm at the point of death. What good could that birthright do me?" Jacob said, "Swear to me today [that you are selling it to me]." And Esau swore to [Jacob] and sold him his birthright. Then Jacob gave Esau the bread and lentil stew, and he ate and drank and rose up and went his way. Thus Esau scorned his birthright as beneath his notice.

Esau was a bad relational strategist.
- He had a poor understanding of his self-worth and value.
- He settled for immediate gratification at the expense of long-term value.
- He did not count the cost of the relationship.

It is common for individuals, organisations and some church leaders not to count the value of what they possess, but to pass it up for instant gratification.

The better option: Joseph and the Butler

In this well-known Bible story, Joseph, although he was in a seemingly disadvantaged position, negotiated strategically with the imprisoned butler of the king. He was clear about his gifting, his ability and his directives to the king. Our gift will always open the way for us and bring us before kings and nobles.

God has given us the gift. It's how we value it and use it to influence and advance his kingdom that is important. Joseph's wise approach paid off at the right time. We must always enter into strategic partnerships with deep reflection and godly wisdom.

A while ago, a notable leader in a high position within the government made a request to visit our local assembly. So we pulled out all the stops to create a memorable visit for this important guest. Since he was influential in political and diplomatic circles, his visit also inspired keen public and media interest.

Knowing well that most invitations to and visits by public figures were guided by motives of political repositioning, I did some quick research to try to find out his reason for coming. Why did he choose us? It became clear that his visit was part of a plan to embrace the ethnic minority churches for political benefit. So we strategized as a team.

We came up with some issues that required attention within our context but which required engagement with our people to bring about a solution. We negotiated for spaces to be created that would enable people from within our local assembly to get involved and contribute in a strategic way. We highlighted some problem areas that the visitor would want to seek solutions for, and then presented him with a team of individuals whose core competencies might actually provide the answers.

God has given us the gift. It's how we value it and use it to influence and advance his kingdom that is important.

Every key leader in government or political office is looking for people and organisations that can make their tenure successful. It is not uncommon for church leaders and heads of organisations to receive invitations from mayors, MPs, governors, commissioners or heads of government. They may want us to visit them, or they may want to visit us.

So it is important to research the reason for the invitation and anticipate how our church or organisation might be able to meet the needs of the political leader. We should also position ourselves to add value to the conversation.

Every key leader in government or political office is looking for people and organisations that can make their tenure successful.

Remember, we cannot make effective change from without. The rule of the game is to navigate a path towards belonging, before we challenge the status quo. We must start from the position of value before we request benefits for our organisation.

CASE STUDY
If only you know what you have, you will not beg for favours
I was once asked for an audience by a young man who ran a successful and growing enterprise with a thriving ministry. The young man had a lot going for him. He was no doubt envied by many people within his generation, and he made the most of his social connections. I looked forward to meeting him

because of the many ways a relationship could benefit both of us.

The young man started by telling me all the things he wanted me to do for him. He was almost pleading with me, thereby placing himself in a position of disadvantage. Little did he know that he carried a lot of value and opportunities that many people would gladly have benefited from. He was about to exchange his chicken for an egg.

I was forced to educate the young man on how to manage relationships of strategic importance. His opening lines needed to be about what he had — not what he wanted. I helped him to identify the numerous chickens in his possession and showed him how to use them as leverage when negotiating for what he did not have.

I told him his first assignment before meeting me should have been to research me and find out the areas in which I was disadvantaged or less empowered — areas in which I could have used his assistance.

I further advised him that his conversation should have begun by highlighting those areas of my need that he could help me with. Such an offer would have compelled me to pay attention to him, and under such a circumstance I would have had to take seriously whatever he might have proposed. This was a classic example of knowing how to get what you need by leveraging what you have.

We must start from the position of value before we request benefits for our organisation.

Move Into Position

SIX

In Strategic relationships, always identify and approach key decision makers and gate keepers where necessary

TYPES OF STRATEGIC PARTNERSHIP

*1. **Political** — with councillors, mayors and MPs*
A church can aim to develop strategic relationships with political leaders within its community and city. All politicians want to win the next election and they need a network of people within their constituency to advance their manifesto. A church with a clear strategic mandate will make itself known to the local councillors, mayors and members of parliament.

The aim is not to be recognised as one of many churches in the area, but to identify ways that the local political machinery will consider the position of our church as advantageous and influential for winning local seats at the election.

Community initiatives include schools, hospitals, prisons, police, help for the homeless, old people's homes and youth organisations. A church can set itself to be a major influencer in decisions that affect different sectors of the local community. A church can become a place of first contact in the community or a place of referral to and from local authorities.

A church with a clear strategic mandate will make itself known to the local councillors, mayors and members of parliament.

A church can equip its members to influence the local schools by directly engaging and creating space for forums on issues regarding local education. Church members can be encouraged to sit on the governing councils of schools, and help to shape decisions that will affect their future.

A church can be visible and acknowledged for hospital visits. It could become a point of reference if patients at the local hospital requested contact from a specific denomination. Some church ministers can apply to become voluntary hospital chaplains who help to create awareness of the sphere of the church.

Working with the police must be a top agenda item for any church that wants to influence its community. Police are out to reduce crime, while a role of the church is to preach righteous living. A clear understanding of the church's role and position in the community means a strategic partnership with the local police would place the church as a point of reference.

A church can equip its members to influence the local schools by directly engaging and creating space for forums on issues regarding local education.

A church could be a major avenue for contact and engagement with the local community, especially a church populated by youth and ethnic migrants. An engaging church might ultimately become a place where the local police come for advice and guidance in the first instance, especially when dealing with crime by migrants from different backgrounds, contexts and cultures.

Such an opportunity allows the church to be a voice and an influence. Some members could be encouraged to become police chaplains and lay visitors to the local justice system.

Many churches have taken the opportunity to minister at local prisons. They have helped their members to become prison chaplains and to influence the inmates' return to normal community life.

A clear understanding of the church's role and position in the community means a strategic partnership with the local police would place the church as a point of reference.

A church that aims to influence its community should be active at the local old people's home. A strategic alliance with the local council which can advise the church on its engagement with the elderly will advance the relational and influential position of that church. Creating a relational event at an old people's home will also refresh, renew and brighten the lives of the elderly and position the church as an oasis of life.

Jesus House London, a Pentecostal church and part of the worldwide Redeemed Christian Church of God, holds an annual event called the "Celebration of Life" for many old people in rest homes within its community.

The event creates an opportunity for local councillors and mayors to affirm their ongoing support for the church and it positions the church as a major player and influencer within the community. A simple but well-planned dinner and dance event, reminiscent of old times, brightens the lives of residents from different old people's homes and revives happy memories for many of them.

2. *Media* — *with the press, generic media outlets, PR persons and other people of influence.*
Many churches know how to tell the story of "dog bites man," but few know how to tell the story of "man bites dog." If a church can learn how to translate its extraordinary events into newsworthy stories, its sphere of influence can be extended in the community.

101

Rarely will a media house publish a story about a church service or about generic church activities. However, every media house needs a story or stories to publish in order to remain relevant. A relational partnership between a church and local media houses through visits and regular communication means those media houses will be happy to publish stories about any of the church's *newsworthy* activities. Media outlets can include radio, newspapers, magazines and local television.

It's not what you know but who you know that translates to influence.

There are times when key figures and personalities visit a church. When such moments come, you can invite the various media houses with whom the church has developed a strategic relationship. But a church must also learn to write its own media releases, and take good photos. A good story accompanied by a good photo can become a feature news item. Take the initiative to write the story and send it in promptly.

A church must aim to deconstruct assumptions and generate public debate on current social issues, without compromising the integrity of the Word. Such discussions and dialogues present the leadership of the church as community influencers so that they become points of reference on theological and social issues.

3. *Festivals and Events* — *Participation and presence at national Christian festivals, and civic and landmark ceremonies.*

The seasons of the Christian calendar are key opportunities for a church to be known as an influencer within its community. It's great to celebrate seasons like Easter, Christmas and New Year "in house," but the church that aims to influence will also inspire its congregation to look outward and engage holistically with its community.

Big events on the Christian calendar are legitimate excuses to create links. They open networks of opportunities that proclaim the ongoing work of the church.

A good "Pancake Tuesday" may not be ideal for black churches but it is important for the English culture. Many churches haven't a clue about "Remembrance Sunday," but it's a point of contact with the community. What about hiring a donkey and asking the kids in the community to ride as actors for Palm Sunday? The story this generates could incorporate a simple expression of the Gospel.

4. *Collaboration* — *with Christian and charitable organisations*

We have seen that strategic partnerships and collaboration are needed because no church can do everything on its own. When a local church organised a "Christmas Lunch on Jesus," little did they know they were starting a movement. This grew into a collaboration of 36 different churches from different denominations working together.

Ultimately it became a franchise, with matching funding from a charitable organisation. That local church became a leading player in an initiative that is being duplicated across the country. That is influence defined.

A small church can collaborate with bigger churches within the community and leverage on the benefits of joint participation and partnership. A bigger church can become a major influencer by inviting smaller churches within the community to come alongside as contributors and participants in initiatives that will jointly affect and advance the community.

Move Into Position

SEVEN

When engaging in strategic relationships, Always think! What do I have to offer?

LEVERAGING STRATEGIC PARTNERSHIPS

Always think: *What do I have to offer?*

Often churches and leaders wrongly assume they have little within their establishment with which to negotiate, few strengths or competences that could advance them as players in strategic relationships.

Regardless of the size of the church, it is important to identify your specific strengths and assets. Here are some institutional assets that could be useful to you, as a church, as you negotiate for strategic partnerships.

MINISTRY OUTLETS — *prayer, music, hospitality, etc.*

A church can position its in-house ministry assets to influence community players and gain leverage. A church might be too small to be acknowledged among other churches and networks in the community but such a church could volunteer to lead prayer support teams for community events. It could influence decisions in regard to community prayer.

No matter how small the church, its voice as an influencer in pioneering prayer initiatives cannot be ignored.

A church can volunteer its music ministry to support local initiatives or create a contemporary band that will be known and invited for events within the community. Because it is presented as a gift to the community, music will open up opportunities for the community to engage with the church. Musical events could be a particular blessing to people who could not otherwise afford to attend them. A community choir might be another way for a church to influence its community.

Love and Joy Choir from Temple of Praise, Liverpool, is a leading church choir that is now regularly booked to perform at major civic and social functions within the city.

Being part of a larger denominational body — the numbers factor
Aristotle said, "The whole is greater than the sum of its parts." Many small churches or parishes belong to, or are affiliated with, established large denominations. It's possible for a church to have fewer than 30 members in its congregation, but when it is engaging in strategic partnership, that number can become an asset. And the small church has the capacity to mobilise thousands of people that are within the reach of the larger denomination.

Being part of a larger denominational body will allow leaders of small churches to negotiate a wider sphere of influence when engaging in strategic relationship at a local or national level.

Professional and gifted human resource pool
A church may offer professionals and gifted individuals as leverage to engage and influence its

111

community. For example, a church once opened its doors for free medical and health checkups for the people in the community. A few professionals in the medical field were able to influence their employers to promote this free health initiative. Another church provided free legal advice for people in their community.

The key factor here is to identify the needs of the community and match them with the resources of the church. Keep in mind these strategic connections have the ultimate aim of making the church a key player and influence in the community.

CHURCH FACILITIES - *Car parks and church halls* An extension of the church facilities may position a church for strategic influence. A church car park can be a point of connection to those in the community who may require a place to park during key events and ceremonies. The church hall or auditorium facilities can be strategically used as a way to pull key stakeholders into the church building and showcase the ongoing activities of the church.

One church opened its building for the local council to use for their meetings and conferences; another offered its auditorium for local beauty pageants and competitions. What is key is that the church is seen not just as a building but as a provider of facilities which furnish the community with a window into its life. Eventually it will influence the decisions of that community.

Generic social initiatives within the church
A church venue may be a meeting point for generic social initiatives. A church once used a section of their building for the Foodbank project. This allowed the community to directly connect the church with this social programme. The church displayed pictures of Foodbank recipients, figures and statistics, and soon became a place of first reference for food allocation in the community.

This was done in conjunction with the council, and the church's influence was maximised when the incumbent mayor nominated the initiative as his charity of the year.

EIGHT

Christmas Lunch on Jesus (CLOJ) an example of collaborative effort of different churches towards a common goal.

POSITIONING FOR STRATEGIC PARTNERSHIP

Do Your Research Diligently
- Gather knowledge about your community and its needs
- Match the needs of the community with what you can offer
- Have a SMART plan

Identify and approach key decision makers and gatekeepers, where necessary. When a strategic partnership is proposed, use the following questionnaire as part of your initial assessment of the opportunity:

117

- Does the proposed partnership contribute to the mission or vision of your church?
- Does the proposed alliance allow the church to achieve its objectives more effectively or efficiently?
- Are there competitive advantages to forming this partnership? For example, would this allow the church to lessen its risks, gain access to a new public or take advantage of a new opportunity that otherwise might not come to fruition?
- Would the partnership be important enough to include in the strategic plan of your church?
- Would the partnership be important enough to continue receiving the support and attention of your leadership team after its formation?
- What would be the key reasons (drivers) for seeking this partnership rather than doing it alone?
- What key objectives might the church achieve through this alliance?
- What channels and mechanisms should the church use to identify a potential strategic partner?
- What are key attributes to look for in a strategic partner?
- How much would the focus of your church attract strategic partners?

- What could be the typical life cycle of the strategic partnership and how would it end?
- Which aspects of the strategic partnership would you expect to work well?
- What barriers would you need to overcome in order to establish such a partnership?
- What aspects of the strategic partnership would be the hardest to work with?

CASE STUDY
Christmas Lunch on Jesus (CLOJ)
by Ngozi Dorothy Molokwu

In 2007 Christmas Lunch on Jesus (CLOJ) was started by Jesus House, a church in North London, as an outreach project for the people in the community. Twenty-five other churches within the borough have since come on board, and so far more than 15,000 hampers have been distributed to residents on low incomes who are in great need and deprivation.

The hampers contain a Christmas turkey and other essentials for a great Christmas lunch — potatoes, carrots, Brussels sprouts, Christmas pudding, chocolates and sparkling juice, to mention a few. Also included are materials giving the recipients more information about the Christmas season and activities by different churches in which they could get involved, such as carol services and nativity plays.

Jesus House has been involved in more than 300 community initiatives within their local borough (Barnet) over the years. As a result, it has strong links with the Barnet Council, the metropolitan police command in Barnet, the Brent Cross shopping centre, Transport for London, and so on.

In order for CLOJ to achieve its objectives, the church had to forge various strategic alliances. The first was with major civic and political leaders. These persons have supported CLOJ over the years and are involved in packing and distributing the Christmas hampers within the borough of Barnet. They include the leader of the Council, the former deputy mayor and her husband, members of parliament, and others. As a consequence of this partnership with local political leaders, the CLOJ team was invited to the House of Parliament by the Barnet MP to be thanked for their work in the community.

Each CLOJ hamper cost £25, but the retail value of its contents was at least £40. The cost savings were made possible through partnerships with various organisations who freely contributed items. Over the years one pharmacy contributed 3000 health monitors, another organisation gave 3,500 Bibles, and another gave hair products from the 2012 London Olympics.

Other alliances have included a High Street bank which has contributed £3500 annually to CLOJ since 2011. Bank staff also participate in the fundraising Sunday service by encouraging the congregation to give to CLOJ.

CLOJ grew from a Barnet-based initiative to become a multi-borough community initiative. It has involved strategic partnerships between churches in Barnet, Brent, Enfield and as far as away as Kent, Dunstable and Merton in the UK.

We look for like-minded churches and organisations with similar goals and beliefs, who have a passion to reach out to the community at large. The purpose of the partnerships is to leverage on one another's strengths. By pooling our resources we can make a bigger impact and reach the less privileged in other communities. Resources shared amongst the partners include the CLOJ operations manual, volunteer training manuals, evangelistic materials and DVDs, and fundraising and marketing materials. Each year, CLOJ attracts more than 250 volunteers from different churches. They work in unity to ensure that families and individuals who are on low incomes or in desperate need have a good meal at Christmas.

CLOJ has grown through various strategic partnerships but one of the most fascinating has been with a church of South African origin. Interestingly, they too were contemplating a scheme to help the less privileged at Christmas, so they contacted CLOJ about the possibility of coming on board as a partner church. It was perfect timing, as CLOJ had recently decided to expand beyond Barnet through community franchises.

The partnership showed to us the importance of churches engaging with all facets of their local community. Doxa Deo, an organisation that CLOJ developed a strategic relationship with, organised a classical concert auction tagged *The Merton Messiah* with the London Festival Orchestra conducted by Ross Pople. They had ties with various Merton personalities, including the Metropolitan police commandant for Merton. He sourced various items for the auction, including a signed picture by former Wimbledon winner Andy Murray, and more than

£10,000 was raised for CLOJ. As a show of support for Doxa Deo, Jesus House bought five tickets at £100 each for key members of the CLOJ team. All volunteers who helped on CLOJ attended free of charge.

Doxa Deo also organised a bike ride to Paris in August 2013 which raised £2000 for CLOJ. An annual bike ride to Paris with Doxa Deo is currently in the pipeline. This would be a great bonding exercise and further strengthen our relationship.

As Jesus House is the operations head office for CLOJ, it is vital that we respond promptly to any request for support that is made by Doxa Deo and other partners. A lack of support could easily breed frustration that could undermine the partnership, so it is important to make other partner churches or franchises feel "we are all in this together." Comments, suggestions and opinions are always welcome, and acted upon quickly to strengthen the relationship.

NINE

Always begin conversations with what you can do to help and how you can provide value from your area of strength and competency.

STEPS IN MAKING STRATEGIC PARTNERSHIP HAPPEN

Write

Having identified the group with whom you want to develop a strategic partnership, write to introduce yourself or your organization. Emphasise what you can offer to add value, and don't bring up any pressing request from your church or organisation. It is important to research your prospective partner and understand their area of need. Then you match this with your area of competence and introduce yourself as a solution bearer and problem solver.

Have an up-to-date website and a clean corporate presentation. Cheap is not often cheerful. It is important to create a positive image, regardless of the size of your church and its need.

Invite

Follow up your letter with an invitation to meet with the prospective strategic partner. If you have your own place of worship, it is worthwhile to make the effort to create an atmosphere that will inspire your guests to see you as a worthwhile future partner. Based on your research about your prospective partner, focus the invitation on what you can do to help that partner in their area of need.

It is important to research your prospective partner and understand their area of need. Then you match this with your area of competence and introduce yourself as a solution bearer and problem solver.

Never present yourself from a position of need, but from a position of helpfulness. If your church does not have a place of worship, arrange to meet at a leading church within your denomination. This helps to paint a picture of success and what the future could look like, as well as giving you credibility as a potential partner.

Visit

Often a letter of introduction or referral may generate an invitation to visit your prospective partner. The same rule applies. Simply do your research on them.

Always begin the conversation with what you can do to help, and how you can bring value from your area of strength and competency.

- Make yourself known to your local councillor, MP and the mayor.
- Offer to be a chaplain to different bodies in your community, for example the local police, hospitals, prisons, and so forth.
- Visit your local media houses.

At strategic meetings remember to:
- Present your ideas with a focus on how the other party can benefit.
- Talk less on what you are going to receive and more on what you have to offer.

If the potential partner is not keen, keep the door open by using the opportunity to affirm their vision, thus cementing a personal relationship of future benefit.

Encourage Others into Strategic Positions

Most church leaders have plenty to do, but when planning for the future of the church you need to encourage your members to think strategically. Encourage them to use their gifts in ways that will benefit the community and bring value to the church's ministry. Such encouragement and teaching must be intentional, and it must be driven from the front.

Always begin the conversation with what you can do to help, and how you can bring value from your area of strength and competency.

Examples of strategic positions of influence
Encourage your church members to work pro-bono in the community. For example:

* *As Justices of the Peace (JPs)* or magistrates if you live in the UK. Anyone can be a magistrate; one doesn't need to be a graduate or a law expert. Magistracy is for lay people who are later tutored on appointment to judge at the local courts. Ask

130

for an application form from your local council or the local magistrates court.

- *As politicians.* Members can become politically active and campaign for political office.
- *As school governors.* Members can make themselves known to the local schools.
- *As directors or trustees for charities and community-based organisations (CBOs)*
- *As participants at local meetings of "Churches Together."* In this they can volunteer for leadership.

Long Term Benefits of Strategic Partnerships

- Your church will become a governing church
- You will be actively involved in major decisions affecting your community
- You will become a community-influencing church
- You will have more opportunities to access grants and gifts from various donors.
- Ultimately the holistic gospel will be preached to all.

FINALLY...

POWERPOINTS

Chapter 1

- In every sphere of work it is important to work out where 20% of effort can lead to 80% of return, while striving for excellence in a few key areas.
- Working with others is about finding a common ground to agree on a **Yes**, and working through differences when there is a **No**.
- Getting to **Yes** is about finding strength in differences, not by simply assuming common needs and experience.

Chapter 2

- Usually it takes more than one person or organisation to effect influence.
- Because the church and the general public keep evolving, alliances will help you to make continuous progress and to stay ahead.
- Fast-growing organisations rely heavily on alliances to improve their operational outcomes.

Chapter 3

- Do not engage in strategic partnerships empty-handed.
- Always position yourself or your organisation from the place of your specific competence or service.
- Successful people invest their time, energy and resources into their core strengths, because from these they get their highest return.

Chapter 4

- You must aim to progress from being just a participant to being a worthwhile contributor and key player, and ultimately a manager.
- Your aim is not just to be voted, appointed and elected onto management boards across the community, but to advance to leadership.

- Partnership with others gives access into research already done, thereby reducing development costs when venturing into new initiatives.

Chapter 5

- Individuals, organisations and most church leaders may not realise the value of what they already possess, and exchange this for instant gratification.
- God has given us gifts. It's how we value them and use them to influence and advance his kingdom that counts.
- Every key leader in governmental or political office is looking for people and organisations that can make their tenure successful.

Chapter 6

- A church with a clear strategic mandate will make itself known to local councillors, mayors, and MPs within its area.
- A church can equip its members to influence local schools by directly engaging and creating space for forums on issues regarding local education.

- Some church ministers can apply to volunteer for hospital chaplaincy, to help create awareness of the sphere of the church.
- A clear understanding of the church's role and position in the community means a strategic partnership with the local police will place the church as a point of reference.
- It's not *what* you know but *who* you know that translates to influence.
- A church must aim to deconstruct assumptions and generate public debate, without compromising the integrity of the Word on current social issues.
- Seasons in the Christian calendar are legitimate excuses to create links and open networks of opportunities that will proclaim the ongoing work of the church.
- A small church can collaborate with bigger churches in the community, and leverage on the benefits of joint participation and partnership.

Chapter 7

- Regardless of the size of your church, it is important to identify your assets and specific areas of strength.

- No matter how small your church, its voice as a pioneer in prayer initiatives cannot be ignored.
- Bcing part of a larger denominational body will allow a small church to negotiate a wider sphere of influence when engaging in a strategic relationship at a local or national level.

Chapter 8

- Match the needs of the community with what you can offer
- Always make sure the partnership is important enough to be included in the strategic plan of the church
- Think through what could be the typical life cycle of a strategic partnership and how it will end

Chapter 9

- It is important to research your prospective partner and understand their area of need. You then match this with your arca of competence and introduce yourself as a problem solver.

- Never present yourself from a position of need but from a position of potential assistance.
- Always begin the conversation with what you can do to help and how you can bring value from your area of strength and competence.
- If the prospective partner is not keen, keep the door open by affirming their vision, thus cementing a personal relationship of future benefit.

- END -

ABOUT THE AUTHOR

Yemi is the CEO of RyA Consultancy Firm, where he delivers strategic advice to leaders. His passion is to discover, build relationship with, and connect leaders with thinkers in relational networks to advance their work.

Yemi is both an Anglican Priest and a Pentecostal Pastor and currently consults as Director "One People Commission" at Evangelical Alliance UK, Associate Director Hope Together UK, Ambassador Compassion UK and Cinnamon Network. Yemi speaks regularly at leadership conferences, churches, corporations, Minister's Conferences and Seminars. Yemi is married to Simi with 4 daughters and 6 sponsored children across the world.